Girl, Embrace IT!

The Cycle And The Method

A 7-Step Method To Embracing and Releasing Your "IT"

Shalimar C. Johnson

Dedication

This book is dedicated to God and every woman who has experienced disappointment or insecurity and needs a release and is bold enough to Embrace IT!

God instructed me to write this book and women in need of a release and a breakthrough motivated me to go through with it.

Table of Contents

Acknowledgements

I would like to thank the Holy Spirit for talking to me and telling me to get this book going. Had it not been for God, I would not have done this.

I would also like to thank my "Girl, Publish It!" supporters for their encouragement throughout this process.

I say THANK YOU to all my friends (you know who you are) for supporting me too.

Preface

When the Holy Spirit pulled on me to write this book, I initially ignored the voice. As time progressed, I began to notice something around me: Women around me started dying (literally and emotionally) at the hands of their abuser. Women started coming to me with questions on how to find a way out of their violent situations or the chaos in their minds. Women began talking to me about the choices they made in relationships and the choices they made in men.

During these moments, I started reflecting on my past and current life. I started considering this book again. The more that I embraced the idea of this book, the more I began to feel weight lifting off me. You see, for a long time and even while writing this book, I was in a place in my life where I felt defeated. I looked around and felt like I had not accomplished anything worthwhile. Yes, I was a parent and that was an accomplishment. But I was single and then married and in distress.

There was no house that I owned to be proud of. No great income to look back on. At points in time, there were no accolades to refer to. I didn't live in the best of neighborhoods. I had vehicles, and they were nice but my credit report showed how many were repossessed. All I saw around me was failure. How could I possibly help anyone out of their situation? How could I be an inspiration? How could I write a book?

How was I supposed to help someone with relationship issues when I was divorcing the man that I married? We weren't living together. I didn't have his support or his presence. I was basically a single woman. No, a man does not define me. But he definitely can compliment me, encourage me, support me, push me and love me. I didn't have that and I felt alone. Being alone wasn't always fun.

So what makes me qualified to write this book? I PERSEVERED! I made a decision to win. I was done with losses. I was done feeling defeated. I was over being depressed. I chose to get more out of life and to live again. I forgave myself and I forgave others. Once I was freed, I became available to God. He was able to work on me and through me. He was able to give me *The Method* (you'll learn more about it later). Through the use of my (this) method, I have successfully helped women from the US all the way to Africa, free themselves from the bondage of unforgiveness.

Introduction

Throughout my life, I struggled in the areas of love and relationships. These relationships included those with family and even friends. In this book, there are two parts. Part One is *The Cycle* and Part Two is *The Method.* In The Cycle, I take you through my journey of love, relationships, disappointment, self-discovery, reality, and release. The Method provides you with 7 steps that I personally use and have helped others use to become free from bondage and forgive-for real. Let me share with you what I discovered were the contributing factors to my failures in love and relationships.

You see, I lost a man that I thought would be my husband. I lost a man who made me feel like no other had. I lost the man who introduced me to love. When I lost him, I lost sight of my worth. I became complacent. I began accepting a lot of things in a relationship that at one point I would never think of accepting. Later on in life, I found myself married and being abused. I knew it was wrong. I knew that he did not love me. But I stayed because I made a vow and I didn't want to disappoint God or confuse my church. Yes, my church (that's another story for a later time). Despite all of that, I still had hope in love.

I was searching for what the man that I lost gave me. The cycle of entertaining unworthy men and embracing unhealthy relationships continued and worsened after he was gone. I set standards, but when they were not met, I figured it was because only the man that I lost could meet them. I thought that since he wasn't making an effort to keep or find me, I could never have his kind of love. I felt like only he possessed what I needed.

The Holy Bible declares in Proverbs 18:22 that, "Whoso findeth a wife findeth a good thing, and obtaineth favour of the Lord." So, in my mind, and according to what I understood, the man was supposed to find me. He was supposed to choose and I, in turn, would choose to say yes or no. Well, I felt like he (the man that I lost or whoever God had for me) wasn't looking in my direction. So, I gave up. Then, there was a point when I had a revelation. This revelation came once I released the hurt. Once I was past the hurt of failed relationships, I realized that I didn't lose the man that I loved. I learned from him. I had to shift the perception that I had of myself and my way of thinking. I stopped searching for who to blame or what I lost and started seeking ways in which I could heal completely because the hurt from "losing him" wasn't the only thing that I needed to heal from. I needed to heal from experiences in my childhood, the reality of a strained relationship with my mom and the feelings of failure as a single mother.

Before I got married, while transitioning from relationship to relationship, I often found myself in a situation where the person I was committed to was the man I kind of liked and not the man that I absolutely loved. I convinced myself to try to love the man who seemed to like or love me more. That concept is how I ended up married to the man that I liked and not the man that I loved. That's a part of how I ended up missing the signs of an abuser and staying in an abusive marriage.

What do you do when you have married the man that you like and not the man that you love? Well, you can suck it up and stay, pack your bags and leave, or tell him what you are going through and see where it takes you. Because surely, cheating is not an option (at least it shouldn't be). As I travelled along my love journey, I made plenty of "love" mistakes. Why? Because I was fueled by defeat and plagued with rejection which led to my constant despair. Whew! What a journey! Once I embraced it and released the mistakes, the pain, the agony and the disappointment, I was able to love myself again, which, in turn, allowed me to be available to love and be loved by a man again.

Part One:
The
Cycle
Begins

Our First Moments

It all started in the year of 1997 but got deeper in 1998. I was 17 years old and a senior in high school. It was almost mid-school year, and I was figuring out what I wanted to do once I graduated. During this time, I met a young man whom I never really noticed, but apparently regularly saw. What drew me to him were these red, green, and clear beads that he wore around his neck. Not too long after I noticed it on him, did I begin noticing it on others. So, I felt compelled to find out more about him. I wanted us to be properly introduced. That was the moment when our love journey all began.

What seemed to be a simple connection because of a common interest (the beads) turned into a life-changing love experience that I would never forget. Let me take you to our first moments.

I'm going to give this young man a name. I'll call him **Shawn**. So, the beads that Shawn wore around his neck were of great significance and actually an ingenious idea for a tool that allowed kids to share testimonies and witness to others about Jesus Christ. Those who wore the beads were a part of a group called The G.A.N.G. (God's Awesome New Generation). The group took a stand for Christianity, were not afraid to pray in front of others, had bible study on Wednesday's, held each other accountable for doing what was right and did that and more without apology.

I was impressed with the group but I was more impressed with Shawn. It was a few months later (but it felt like only a few days) and before I knew it, my eyes shifted and I didn't see just **Shawn**. Before even being formally introduced, I saw this young man who was on fire for God, held an intelligent conversation, played one of the sexiest instruments (the saxophone), was in the school band and was FINE. Ok, I know. I was full of lust. Hey, I was 17 and just really learning about God, purpose, and destiny. Don't judge me.

Moving along. I was walking through the hallway and saw the ONE guy in the school who was known as "The Preacher". He had beads too! I was too afraid to approach Shawn, so instead, I decided to approach The Preacher. He would basically talk to anyone. You just had to be prepared to either hear a word, be prayed for or get rebuked.

I mustered up enough courage and asked him about his beads. He invited me to one of their after-school meetings which happened to be the same day. It was perfect because we got out of school at 2:30 and my mom usually didn't get me until close to 4:00 and the meeting was from 3:00-3:45. I used the payphone to call my mom to make sure she wasn't coming early. I was bubbling with excitement on the inside because my mom was going to pick me up a little late. I was ready to head to the meeting. Now, I was intrigued by the beads, but if the truth be told, I wasn't going to the meeting solely to hear about Jesus. I was going to find out more about Shawn. Hey, don't judge me.

To my surprise, I didn't focus much on Shawn at all because the meeting was really good. We broke out into groups. The guys were with the guys and the girls were with the girls. So much for my plans. Isn't that like God? He will show you that it's not about following your plans, but about fulfilling His.

Reasonably, Shawn and I began having plenty of conversations about "The G.A.N.G." since we both attended the meetings and I now had my own beads. For a while, that's what our conversations were primarily about. However, when we discovered that we had other things and interests in common, we had even more to talk about. We had another reason to be around each other.

By now, I think you know that I found Shawn to be attractive. At this point in our friendship, I started to think that he might find me attractive too. Not because he told me or alluded to it, but because I just had this innate feeling that what we had was more than just a simple common connection. Ok. It was *that* feeling mixed with the fact that I wanted him to like me. Just follow me.

The Royal Court

So, I entered a pageant, The Royal Court Pageant, during the school year and it had finally come to an end. (I actually participated in several pageants throughout high school). This pageant consisted of a series of events that were hosted over several months such as a talent show, writing competitions, community service initiatives and more. Shawn was there through it all. By this time, Shawn and I had expressed a deep interest in each other (which did include a little Jesus), but we were DEFINITELY headed in the direction that I wanted. We had gotten to a place where each other's support and encouragement was not only wanted but needed.

I was in drama class at school getting prepared to leave for a performance at another location when I got a call that the winner was determined and would be announced at an event that evening. We were never told exactly when the winner would be announced, just that it would be at one of the last three scheduled events, and this one was it. I made it to the event and I was super nervous. Once the judge said, "Good Evening family and friends, it is now time to announce our Royal Court," I quickly focused my mind and attention on other things, just in case my name wasn't called. You see, I didn't want anyone to see the look of defeat or shame on my face if I lost. I figured if I was able to preoccupy myself with something else, it may not be noticeable.

The judge started with Little Mister and Miss, then Junior Mister and Miss and then finally Mister and

Miss. The first name that was called was not mine. Whew! That meant that I was either the winner or the runner up. I wanted to be the winner. I worked hard to get that spot.

The judge said the second name and…it…was… MINE! I was disappointed but excited at the same time. At least I was on the court. Me not winning the ultimate title did not stop me from pursuing other goals. I was still focused on determining what I wanted to do after high school. I still worked on getting enough community service hours to earn a cord to wear at graduation. I still wanted to save and earn enough money to finally buy a flip cellphone- no more pager for me! Another goal was to be with Shawn. Because I was so "in to" Shawn, I put a brief pause on those other goals and focused more on him. That list and Shawn were the only things that I had on my mind. He had my full attention until this happened…

It was early one Saturday afternoon. I had just hung up with MY man (yes, we made it official), but he called me back about 30 minutes later. My mom called my name to let me know that Shawn was on the phone. In my head I was thinking, "Aww, he misses me already".

Well, before my mom handed me the phone, she shared some information with me. My mother explained to me that she had a conversation with one of the ladies that served as a judge for the Royal Court Pageant. In this conversation, the lady admitted to and filled my mom in on the fact that the judges had cheated. Yes! They cheated. I actually won! My mother told me about the entire conversation and I was infuriated. The next question from the judge was: "What do you want to do?" Followed by, "Do you want to meet with the committee?"

My mother handed me the phone. (Yes, my man was waiting patiently on the phone and heard me and my mom's entire conversation.) Shawn shared with me that he had become aware of the cheating, too. He and I talked about it and he asked me what I wanted to do. (He was so assuring and comforting.) A part of me wanted to go off on the ladies; another part of me was indecisive. I was indecisive because I thought that by them making an announcement about a month after the initial announcement of the winners, it would tarnish the image of The Royal Court Pageant and damage the integrity of the judges to come.

I talked to my mom and she didn't ask me what I wanted to do. She *told* me to just leave it alone. Huh? Really? Since I was not going to outright disobey my mother, I said nothing. I went on knowing I was truly the Queen, yet, pretended like I was not.

Since Shawn was treating me like a Queen anyway, I quickly forgot about the title that was stolen from me. Shortly after, I realized how much winning meant to the one that was crowned the Queen and began to feel a little bit better about my decision to listen to my mother and say nothing. God was working on me with a quality that I would find myself using quite often in my adult life. I just didn't know it yet.

The Experience

By the time I was dating Shawn, I had only had one serious high school relationship. Well, at least it was serious to me. I prided myself on being loyal even though my boyfriend was a senior when I was a sophomore. I knew he would probably forget about me when he went to college or at least not be faithful. He was tall, light-skinned (this was a big deal back then), and he played football. He was going to a well-known college several miles away. I'm talking about the kind of miles that would cause you to say "NO" to a drive there.

Me and "Mr. Light-skinned" dated until my junior year of high school. By the time I got to the end of my junior year of high school, it was clear that his interest in me dwindled. Although I was loyal and faithful, that was not enough for him (he had gone to college by this time). I mailed him a lengthy letter expressing my feelings and decision to part ways- even though he probably already had. That was the end of that relationship, which was good while it lasted. But it opened a window of opportunity for Shawn. The best opportunity I'd had thus far when it came to relationships.

Shawn and I did almost everything together. We talked for hours, laughed for days, and gazed into each other's eyes for what seemed to be decades. I felt something with him that I had never felt before. I thought things about him that I had never thought before. Was it love? Only time would tell.

He would open doors for me. He would offer his last to me. He would even call just to talk to my mom. I was semi-jealous. Semi. He would give me space, but not too much. He would pray with me and for me. He would have devotion with me and hold me accountable for my actions. He would take me to church and take me to meet his family. I met aunts, cousins, brothers, mother, father—I mean the whole family. He was amazing. He showed me love.

Shawn was the kind of guy who was comfortable in his skin. He may have been considered conceited by others, but to me, he was just confident. He loved to dress nice and smell good and so did I. For these reasons, he always wanted to take pictures together, dress in similar colors, and represent each other together or in each other's absence well. He would often say, "We represent each other everywhere we go". I understood and believed that.

One day, we were riding in his car and he asked me about what I desired to do when we graduated from high school. I told him that I was going to take two years to pursue my acting career and move to New York and attend a conservatory college for film and television. I returned the question. He told me that he was staying in the state and would be attending an HBCU. It was the same school that my grandmother attended. He encouraged me to pursue my dreams and promised me that he would stay with me on my journey. I was in "love heaven". I thought to myself, "Is this real? Is he saying that he will stay with me forever? I'm officially in love. It could NOT get any better than this".

He began to tell me his plans. Remember, I told you that a part of his "fine-ness" was the fact that he played one of the sexiest instruments. Well, when he went to college, he was going to be in the marching band. It was something about an HBCU marching band that would make even the ugliest guy fine. He talked about the degree that he wanted to get as well. But the part that he said that really got me was when he told me that I was in his plans. If I could melt from his words, I would have completely disappeared. That meant so much to me. And I knew he was being true and sincere. Honey, that man was going nowhere, and neither was I. At least that was the thought at the time.

He Put A Ring On It

The end of our senior year was rapidly approaching. We were experiencing teenage dating bliss. We were officially in love. We were not ashamed of PDA (within reason), we couldn't sleep without hearing each other breathing on the other line, we had to talk at least 3 times a day and we HAD to hang up saying, "I love you". We hated hanging up and so we went through rounds of "You hang up", "No, you hang up first", "Babe, you hang up", "Nope" and so on.

Everything about him was amazing to me. Heck, he was so amazing that even his fingernails were wonderful. The way he would look at me captivated me. He would draw me in like you're drawn into a well-directed suspense movie. His kiss was so gentle. He was so endearing. He was the epitome of a gentleman.

Now, was everything always perfect? No. We had disagreements but we never ended a day without getting things resolved. Our disagreements were void of name calling, cursing, or any physical violence. One thing that he made sure of was that we made amends. And we always did. Well, in the beginning at least. I'll tell you about that later.

Back to blissfulness... He would do this little forehead kiss. I want to say that he got it from a movie. It really doesn't matter though. Because I loved it! Even when I reminisce, I smile. He was good for getting me little sweet nothings that meant everything. It could be a letter that he wrote, a poem that he found or a picture collage of us that he created. Everything had thought behind it.

One afternoon, he called the house to see if I was home. He asked my mom (as he always did) if he could come and pick me up. She said yes. We went riding around. We had nowhere in particular to go. So, I thought. We ended up at a park. We got out of the car and walked around the park holding hands and talking about whatever we wanted to. We finally stopped to sit. And then it happened. He looked at me and asked me if I loved him. I said yes. He told me that he loved me too. He asked me if I was sure that I wanted to be with him. I then asked him why. His response was, "I can't seem to function without you. I can't imagine life without you. I know that we will be apart when we go to school and that will be hard. But I am willing to take that chance on you and on us. I am willing to sacrifice and make sure that it works". Immediately I told him that I had never felt the way he made me feel and I wanted that feeling with him and only him forever.

Right then he said, "We are too young to get married. And my mom would probably kill me if I told her we were engaged. But (he pulled out a ring box and got on one knee), will you promise me that you will be committed to us, love me, be with me, encourage me, stay with me? Then, I said, "Yes! Yes!" He placed the ring on my finger symbolic of my promise. But honey, no one could tell me that I wasn't engaged. Again, I thought: "Is this guy real?" I felt like all that I needed was him. At that moment, I was trying to change my plans. I considered switching schools and following him. But what about my dream? Besides, he was onboard. We sealed the promise

with a kiss and went on with our day. I was excited
and scared to tell my mom about the ring. I had the
kind of momma that noticed everything and absolutely
DID NOT allow anything in her house that she was
not aware of- even if it was a ring on MY finger. I was
so in love that the fear was gone soon.

Off To College

The day had come and it was time for Shawn to go off to college. Guess what Shawn did? He wrote my mother a letter asking her for permission to allow me to travel with his mother to take him to college. In the letter, he explained all the plans: where we would be staying, who I'd be in the hotel room with and the stops that we were making along the way. He ended the letter with a promise to her that I would be well taken care of and would return just as she sent me. Oh, the things he would do for me.

I had a blast! We ate dinner as a family. We went to a water park and enjoyed each other's presence. We made countless promises to each other to stay connected, to always write and to remain faithful. I helped his mom put his dorm room together. I didn't do any of these things with the boyfriend that I had before Shawn. I experienced a lot of firsts with Shawn and I wanted those experiences for a lifetime. While I was with him during one of the most important transitions in his life, we didn't want to leave each other's side. We loved being in each other's presence.

You see, at this time, there was no Facebook, there was no Instagram or Snapchat or Twitter. We didn't have video chat options. We barely had cell phones and the internet. But there was Myspace, though. We did have email. The disposable camera was my friend. I bought so many that I should have had stock in Fujifilm. Oh, and I cannot forget about the countless phone cards that I had to purchase just to make long distance phone calls. (Yes, there was an extra cost to make long distance phone calls back then.)

The ride back home was long. I think I slept the entire time. I was missing him so much. The reality of his absence was becoming clear. The need to stay connected was more prominent and the fact that a long-distance relationship was not going to be easy was becoming a reality that I was not ready for. Once I got home, I went to my room, closed my door, laid on my couch and cried. (Yes, there was a couch in my bedroom.)

Later that evening, Shawn called me. We talked for hours. He told me about his first day and his plans for the week. Guess what his plans included? Me! Yes, me. He missed me just as much and decided to take the Greyhound bus and come to my house. He told me to hang up and not answer the phone when it rang. He wanted my mother to answer so that he could talk to her about staying at our house for a couple of days. To my surprise, she said yes. So, three days after we dropped him off at college, I was going to be able to spend two more days with him. My heart was full.

I must have looked out the window every five minutes expecting to see him pull up. He was taking too long. Finally, a yellow cab drove up and stopped. The door opened (almost as if in slow motion), I saw a leg step out of the door, then a body. Could it be him? I was on the third floor and it was hard to tell. Finally, I saw a face and it was him! I quickly looked at the mirror to make sure that my hair was right and I looked pretty for him. Everything was just right. I wanted him to come to the door, but time seemed to move too slowly. So, I opened the door, ran down the stairs and there he was. We hugged each other so tightly. Then he said "Babe, hurry up. I didn't tell my mom that I was going to be here. I don't want anyone to see me". I grabbed his hand and quickly walked up the stairs.

He greeted my mom with a warm hug, hello and thank you and she did the same. We went to my room, sat on the couch, and watched T.V. I wanted to lay on his shoulder or his lap. I even wanted to lay in his arms but he respected my mom and her house. He didn't want her to feel disrespected by us displaying too much affection and causing her not to feel comfortable leaving us alone. He also didn't want her to decide not to allow him to come over again.

The respect was to the point that when it was time to sleep, he kept the room door open and light on, put a chastity blanket between us and slept at the foot of the bed. When we had our alone time, void of my mother's presence, we walked around the apartment complex and by the lake. We relaxed in the Jacuzzi and competed against each other in the gym- *I let him win*! I knew that our time was going to come to an end but we needed those two extra days. Both of us were stressed out. Seeing him helped ease my anxiety. When he got in the cab to go back, I didn't want him to go but his visit was just what I needed to hold on a little longer.

It was finally time for me to go off to college. I was excited. I was about to embark on a journey called "finding myself" and I was ready. I was ready to be on my own. I was ready to make decisions and create memories. I was ready to get settled 1,000 miles away from home. I was ready for New York City! I knew my roommate because I attended a summer intensive at the college that I was going to during my junior year of high school. So, I knew at least one person. She made it to our studio apartment first. It was nice seeing her but a part of me wished that it were Shawn there instead. Honestly, considering what I knew about him, I thought that he might have been there to greet me. I mean, he was full of surprises.

Of course, I called him once I got settled and talked to him about my travelling experience. We talked about what New York looked like, how nervous I was about school and definitely how much we missed each other. This man even talked to my roommate and asked her to look out for me and make sure that we looked out for each other. He told her that I was important to him and that he needed me in his life. He explained to her that he was concerned because New York City was a big, fast-paced place and since he was not there to protect me, he wanted her to look out for me. Could I ask for more?

I Miss You So Much- But How Could You Leave Me?

Shawn and I finally got settled in school but the stress of each other's absence was beginning to take over. We decided that it was time to plan to visit one another. I decided to come first. I was so excited! I was going to see my man, but I was also going to have the opportunity to tour an HBCU. You see, I attended a conservatory college in New York City, and I was a minority. There were no fraternities or sororities. There were no assemblies or sports games to attend. It was film and television every day and that was it. Hence, a conservatory college. So, there were multiple reasons why I wanted to be there.

I finally landed and checked my mirror to make sure my face was clean and my hair was perfect. I had on a black cotton pencil skirt and a black ¾ sleeve fitted shirt, black heels and micro braids. I adorned my body with Victoria Secret's Pear Glace lotion and body spray and accentuated my lips with MAC's Lipglass. I was ready to greet my man. I walked down the aisle gracefully holding on to my Coach tote bag and stopped at the conveyer belt, waiting for my luggage. I soon felt this warm presence behind me. I immediately knew it was Shawn. He pulled my hair from the side of my neck and kissed me softly. I knew that touch all too well. I knew for sure it was him. I turned around and there he was!

We embraced each other in a way that seemed angelic and in slow motion. We didn't care about who was watching or whose way we were in. We waited months for that moment, and no one was going to interfere. Finally, we were ready to let each other go for a moment, leave the airport and head home. But before we left, he sealed our embrace with a forehead kiss (something he would always do).

Shawn was in the process of flipping a house and it wasn't at a point that he felt comfortable with me staying there. So, we stayed at one of his friend's houses one night, his cousin's house the second and the rest of my stay was at the house that he was fixing up. The first night of my stay was when the security, trust, and faith that I had in this man changed.

When I walked into his friend's house (we will call him Tim), I was greeted with open arms by his family. His parents were preparing to leave and go out of town shortly after I arrived. So that would leave me, Shawn, Tim and Tim's cousin (who was about 6'3" 250 pounds and fresh out of jail) at the house. I had only talked to Tim over the phone. This was our first time meeting in person. He seemed to be a pretty cool guy.

Tim's parents gathered us in the family room, laid down a few rules and expectations for all of us to follow and left for their trip. While still in the family room, Tim began to share with me the fact that he was about to be on the same journey as Shawn and I were with his girlfriend and wanted some words of encouragement and insight. I began to share with him how hard it was to be apart from the one you love. I also shared with him how Shawn and I argued and made up, agreed to disagree, laughed and cried, looked back on moments and fell in love all over again. I shared with him that we had to make a decision to stick it through and remember the commitment that we made to each other. I told him how Shawn giving me a ring and me accepting it was one of the best decisions we could have ever made because it held us accountable. It served as a reminder of why we decided to be together. I also shared with him that I was only going to be in my program for two years and I was going to enroll where Shawn was to be closer to him. I gave him words of encouragement and told him that it would work out if they both tried. Shawn heard us talking from the other room and apparently, he wasn't pleased.

He came into the family room with an angry disposition, said to me, "Man, I'm leaving" and walked out. I quickly walked out behind him and asked him what was wrong. He said to me in a loud voice, "You should have never told him about our issues. Why would you share something like that? He doesn't need to know that we argue at all. That's none of his business. I'm out!" and he left.

He left me with the friend that I just met and this big brawly man that I had never met who was fresh out of jail. I grabbed the keys to his mom's van to go on a hunt to find him. Tim asked me to calm down and not to take the car. Instead, he drove me and turned wherever I told him to turn. Then, I spotted it. I spotted his dark green 2-door car parked in the driveway of someone's house. Then I heard his friend Tim mumble "Shawn, why'd you go there? I knew he was going to her house". Her house? Whose house? Who is "her"? These were the questions going through my mind. I was too hurt to react that I simply asked Tim to take me back to his house.

Once we got back, he was trying to assure me that Shawn would be back. He just needed time to breathe. I went into the bedroom that was set aside for me, locked the door, put a chair up against it and laid in the bed and cried. I kept looking at my watch as the hours went by and he still had not returned. Finally, around nine o'clock the next morning, I heard someone fidgeting with the doorknob. I woke up puzzled as I was not sure if it was Tim, Tim's cousin or Shawn. By this time, I had a cellphone and so did Shawn. Shawn didn't call me, so I thought it was someone trying to get in and do something to me. Then I heard a deep voice in a low volume say, "Babe, it's me. It's Shawn". I rolled my eyes, covered my head with the covers and ignored him.

He wouldn't leave the door alone. He insisted that I open the door because he was not going to stop and if he had to, he'd figure out a way to open it anyway. I decided to get up, move the chair and open the door. I didn't open it all the way though. I only cracked it open. He came in, locked the bedroom door behind him, laid in the bed with me, wrapped his arms around me and apologized for leaving. He explained that he was hurt because he felt like I was talking negatively about him. All of that might have worked, if I didn't see his car parked in the driveway at "her" house.

I looked at him and said, "I was only here a couple of hours and because you didn't like what I said, you left me here with two men that I do not know. One who just got out of jail and the other I just met today. You would not answer your phone and you raised your voice at me. Everything that you are telling me now, you could have said to me last night". I promised Tim that I wouldn't tell Shawn that he took me driving around and that he said he was at a girl's house and I kept my word. But I did tell Shawn that I left and went looking for him. I asked him whose house it was that he was at. He was shocked and speechless. Then he told me it was his homeboy's house that he went to so he could clear his mind. "Really? All night? From ten o'clock in the evening until nine the next morning?", I said. I was not buying it and I told him that.

Despite that though, he kept telling me how sorry he was and that he would never do that again. That he was upset and embarrassed and didn't know how to handle it. I told him that I was ready to go back to New York and that I needed time to myself. I went outside and called my friend. I told her what happened and she was in disbelief. She did suggest that I think things through and consider his apology. I did rethink and decided to stay. Me staying did not mean that I wasn't going to or couldn't forgive him or that I saw nothing wrong with what he did. But what I should have done was stood my ground and let it be known that what he did was a big deal and the fact that he could just leave me in those conditions was not a display of love even though he felt like he could trust those guys. What I did not realize at the time, was that experience was the beginning of the cycle of me keeping my mouth shut about hurt and disrespect by a man and allowing men to do whatever they wanted to do to me emotionally.

<u>The Cycle Continues...</u>

After the incident during my last visit with Shawn, we remained an item. We decided to make our long-distance relationship work and cross the bridges as they came. With a clear understanding that they would come.

Communication was the key component in our relationship. I am not speaking so much about verbalizing things as I am about making sure that we emailed, wrote and talked as often as possible. This was vital because that was all we had since we were hundreds of miles away from each other.

We lived in a time where there was no social media. Cell phones were advancing and becoming more affordable for more people. But you had to pay per minute for every call that was out of your calling area plus the monthly cost of the service. Calling cards were more cost effective at the time. Remember, we were college students and though our parents were there to pick up some slack, they didn't pick up everything.

I needed to hear his voice while I looked at a photo of him. It made me feel like he was closer than he really was. I needed to hear him tell me that he loved me so that my day would go smoother. I needed to hear words of encouragement and have our daily devotion so that I could feel like we went to church service together. But, for some reason, he was not answering my calls anymore. I was not getting any responses to the text messages that I sent- those were $0.25 each for the record.

I began to wonder if something happened to him. Because surely, he was not ignoring me. He loved me too much. Right? One week went by. No answer. Two weeks went by. No answer. Finally, midway through the third week, he answered his phone. This is how it went:

Shawn: "Hey, Babe."

Me: "Hey Babe?!" I exclaimed. "What do you mean? I have called you for weeks. I left you dozens of text messages and you responded to none of them! Where were you? Why didn't you answer or call me back?"

Shawn: "I didn't realize that I hadn't talked to you. I've been really busy. You know that I have to practice all day and I have class and I'm trying to work. I'm at a game right now. I just got a chance to answer your call."

Me: "I get all of that. I work nights from 5-9 on weekdays and 9-6 on weekends. I go to school during the week from 8-3 and rehearse in between classes and work. Yet, I still make time to call you at the least. I'm over the excuses. If I can make time, so can you. You push and press for what you want. If you can't make time for me, then you need to rethink what you want to do as it concerns me."

Meanwhile, I hear a young lady's voice in the background saying, "Shawn, Baby, are you coming?"

Me: "Who was that?"

Shawn: "Babe. I don't know why she said that. I have to go. I'll call you when I leave from here."

At this point I really felt like I was a fool to even want to still be with him. But Shawn was all that I knew. I could not just let him go like that. I waited all night for his call. He NEVER called me back. At that point, I made up my mind to begin the process of getting over him and moving on. Besides, I had quite a few men that expressed interest in me that I did not give the time of day to because I was committed to Shawn.

The Visit

About a week later, Shawn called me and apologized for not calling me sooner. I expressly stated that I was hurt, ashamed, sad and DONE. He asked me to just give him a chance. He told me that he purchased a bus ticket and he was coming for his Thanksgiving break. Like really? He just made plans and told me what he was going to do. Initially, I was thoroughly agitated but I thought about it and figured it would be a good idea. Him coming would be a way for me to know if I was truly over him or if the only reason why I was able to deal with our break-up was because he was "out of sight-out of mind".

The day finally came for him to arrive. I got on the train and made my way to the bus station. As soon as I saw him it was like nothing bad ever happened. I quickly forgot about the lack of communication, the possible cheating, what he did when I visited him, EVERYTHING. All that I felt was this tingle in my stomach, a surge of energy in my heart and a desire to hug and kiss him to no end. I felt love.

We made our way to my apartment and got settled. Later on that evening, we took a stroll through Times Square. It felt like it was supposed to feel. We held hands, we laughed, we weren't afraid of a little PDA. We were two college freshmen venturing down a journey called life with a desire to continue and end the journey together.

The next day came and I had to go to work. I made sure that there was enough food for him to eat while I was gone, made him some lunch, headed out the door and got on the G train for work. I missed him as soon as he left my eyesight. All I could do was think about him at work and anxiously anticipate our reunion.

My workday was finally over and I walked down Madison Avenue with extreme excitement. I hopped on the F train, then the A and lastly the G. I walked down what seemed to be the longest block ever, opened my front door and I was met with dimmed lights, photos of me and him and dinner on the table. We danced to the music in our heads without a care in the world. This was enough for me to know that it had to be an "us".

The Departure

The day came for Shawn to go back to his "second home" (mine was declared his first home). It was bitter-sweet. We began packing all his belongings and I began to cry internally (I could not let him see me all broken up). Then he asked me a question that changed my life forever. He asked me what I wanted to do. He wanted to know if we were going to be together or not. I knew that the answer was to be together but I needed him to know that he could no longer treat me like he did. I needed him to know how it felt to sit around and wait on the one that you are in love with to reach out to you. I wanted him to understand that if it happened again, it was over for real. I was comfortable in these feelings because my intentions were pure.

So, I told him that by the time he made it back to his destination, I would call him and let him know what I decided. Immediately, he told me that he was not going to wait on me and I needed to give him an answer right then; that he was not going back without knowing where we stood. I, in turn, told him that it did not work like that. That he could not dictate when I responded. I also told him that he needed to know and understand how it felt to have to wait. I promised him that I was going to tell him as soon as he made it back.

The trip on the train to the bus station was long and quiet. He did not want to hold my hand. He didn't want to be embraced in any way. He barely even looked at me. Once we reached the last train, he told me that he wanted to ride alone. He said that since I didn't give him an answer, he was done and not to wait for a call as he was not going to call me. He told me not to bother calling him because he was not going to answer. I was devastated and mad at the same time. I knew he was serious. The train doors were closing and I quickly got out and watched him through the window as the train began to move.

<u>Coping</u>

The next few days, weeks, months, were the worst I had experienced since having to keep my mouth shut about officials lying about who won for the pageant I was in. I was so hurt. Receiving a phone call from one of the judges admitting that they cheated and finding out that I actually won, coupled with my mom telling me to leave things alone and say nothing was gut-wrenching. Man, that hurt. But this hurt was a different kind of hurt. It went deeper, it pierced my heart harder. I was lost.

Shawn really meant that he was not going to answer the phone. I must have called him 50 times and he did not answer. Let me mention the fact that he didn't call me either. Reality set in that he was done. Then anger began to take over. How could he just let me go like that? Did he forget all the things that he did? I thought that he loved me. That I was the one. We experienced so many firsts together. We were supposed to be each other's last.

I finally accepted the absence of Shawn in my life as my new reality. I slowly began to entertain other men and I finally mustered up the courage to make it official with another man. He was the closest to Shawn I could get. He was much older than me, but when I was with him, he reminded me of Shawn. So, I figured it was a perfect connection.

My new beau exposed me to quite a few things that I would never forget. He showered me with love, diamonds, glass flowers (so they would last forever), gold, expensive dinners, constructive criticism, slow dances in the middle of the night, flowers and balloons just because, the list goes on. We decided to move in together. This was a first for me. But, it was a first that I was willing to experience. When the day came that he told me it wasn't going to work and that I needed to move out, it took me by surprise. I was so confused. I truly did not see that coming.

You see, I experienced "first's" with this guy too. The major first was the fact that we lived together. I had never lived with a man before. The only man that I shared a roof with was my brother. My mother told me that he was going to leave me with my bags at the door and she was right. He had the upper hand. He had money. Yet again, I was lost. I thought the "new reality" of me and Shawn's breakup was something. Man, I now had a serious "new reality".

I gave the experience with Shawn a name. I did this so that I could make a distinct separation in order to stop blaming myself for our breakup. I called it being "Shawn'd". Being "Shawn'd" meant that I was mistreated, misled and left to figure things out on my own. At the point when I was processing this "new reality" with the man I lived with, I felt like I was being "Shawn'd" all over again. I began to question myself. I wondered if I was the issue. If I sucked at relationships. I mean, I gave of myself all that I could give. Despite insecurities, I opened up to these men. I let them into a personal and private place just to end up alone. It was during this time that I started to change my view on my value. My concerns about my value started with Shawn and continued with every relationship I encountered thereafter.

<u>Go Away</u>

As time progressed, I entered several relationships. I finally decided to marry one of the men that I dated. One of the primary reasons that I decided to marry that man was because I became a single parent and I wanted my son to experience living in a home with a mother and a father. I would have never thought that I would be covering up bruises, wiping blood and staying in hotels just to be safe. Once I was finally at the point of ending that marriage, Shawn popped up.

We would talk regularly. We even met up. I really desired for us to talk about being in a relationship but we never did. He did tell a coworker that I was "the one he let get away" though. I really thought that there was a chance for us to start where we left off. Then, he disappeared. He stopped answering my calls, he stopped calling me. No more texting, no more Facetime, nothing. I began to wonder if he only entertained me for vengeance. How did he just leave me hanging like that again?

So, there I was, entangled with insecurities and tied to rejection all while feeling alone. I was "Shawn'd". I was so torn. I was officially done with men. At this point, I was a single mother of two- a boy and a girl- and all I wanted was to be the best mother to them and strengthen my relationship with God. I was content with where I was in life at this point. But, as soon as I was in a place of contentment, Shawn found me again. Because I had not released him from my heart, I opened up and let him in my ear and allowed him to penetrate my heart. The problem was that my heart was still open to him and this was a dangerous place to be in.

For a long time, I thought that if I didn't dwell on the idea or memory of a person or a thing, that I was over them or it. I have come to find out how far from reality that thought is. When Shawn resurfaced, it was hard to ignore him. My problem was that I was holding on to the Shawn that I knew long ago. I remembered him for who he was when I was in love with him. He sounded the same, he pretty much looked the same, so in my mind (though I knew with time came change), he was the same.

It seemed as if every time I was in a vulnerable place or had made up my mind to end a relationship, he would pop up. I would receive a text message with a simple but dangerous "hello". He would call me just to tell me that I was on his mind. He would send me a message with a recording of our favorite song or a picture of him. Sometimes I would respond, other times I wouldn't. Then, like before, everything would just stop. I thought about changing my number, but part of me figured that I shouldn't give him that much control to cause me to alter my comfort in any way. But the truth is, I really wanted to be connected to him in some way. I still wanted access to him. Eventually, I finally had enough. Of course, it happened AGAIN. I received another call. This time I went off:

Shawn: "Hey"

Me: "Hey? Seriously!"

Shawn: "What? I was just saying hello"

Me: "Why? What's your goal here? One minute we are on a roll conversing back and forth. Then the next minute you disappear and don't answer my calls. Then, you send me sweet little messages out of the blue. You tell me that you want me to come home and coming home means coming back to you. I tell you that I was open to that idea and then you stop responding to my calls and my messages. I told you that I was moving on from my previous relationship and though I didn't want to jump into anything, I felt like we needed to explore what was going on because for some reason, we are still connected. And after ALL of that, you disappear and now, you wanna call me and say hello? I'm done with the run-around!"

Shawn: "So you're supposed to be going off on me?"

Me: "You know what…?"

Shawn: "My badd. I didn't know all of that."

Me: "Come on now. Yes you DID! I told you. And since you just disappeared, I decided to put you in my past. So now I'm moving forward. You had plenty of opportunities and you chose not to take up on them. I'm not doing this with you anymore."

Shawn:" Alright. Sorry to bother you."

After all of that you would think that was it. IT WASN'T! He reached out to me AGAIN! - several months later. And of course, it was at a time when I was vulnerable and ending a relationship. So, I began to think that it was a sign and not necessarily a warning or a setup. I took the doggone bait - AGAIN.

I kept asking myself what was wrong with me. Why wasn't I able to shake him? I prayed so hard and asked God to remove him from my heart, to sever any ties, to move him out of my life. It felt like the more I prayed, the more I couldn't seem to get him out of my system.

The Revelation

It was early one Sunday morning, and I was really down in my soul. I felt like I had not accomplished much in life. I felt like I failed as a mother. I felt burdened by what my children were exposed to due to the choices I made in men. I had two children, no husband and a man named Shawn who kept playing with my emotions. I was receiving Medicaid and food stamps; I had no college degree and was living a life that I never envisioned. I felt like I was in bondage in my own home. I felt ugly, used up and helpless. I was tired. The last time that I felt that way, I asked God to take me away. I wanted to fall asleep and never wake up. Well, I am still here which means I have work to do.

As I cried (literally) out to God, I asked him to reveal to me what my weaknesses were. I asked Him to help me understand why it was so hard for me to let people or men go. Why would I stick around and deal with a person who'd just use me with no hesitation and treat me like crap? I had asked Him this question before, but my point of brokenness and despair was at a higher level this time around and I *finally* heard Him answer. I'm sure God answered me before though. Sometimes God answers us but because we are not in the right place spiritually, we don't hear Him.

When God answered me, He showed me when the cycle started. He took me to a place when I began accepting whatever came my way. He showed me when I started to feel like what I did wasn't good enough. He showed me when the idea of doing whatever I had to in order to please someone or make them happy became my reality. For a long time, I thought the cycle started when Shawn left me alone. But in actuality, my experiences with Shawn and other men were just contributing events to a way of thinking that was created long before I met them. Where did God take me? He took me to my childhood.

Children have this sense of love and forgiveness that exists because their souls are so pure. Most children want to make mom and dad so proud that no matter what mom or dad may say or do, all they want is love and approval from them. Children are even so eager to have friends that they often let friends say or do whatever to them just to have a friend. Well, as a child, I was fueled by my mother's approval. I was the average child. Sometimes I obeyed and sometimes I didn't. But regardless of what state of mind I was in, my ultimate goal was always to please my mom.

God revealed to me that the cycle of accepting whatever came my way started then- as a child. There were instances in my life where my mother's response was emotionally hurtful. I don't believe that she always intended to be hurtful. Regardless of how harsh she was, she was my mother, and, in my mind, there was nothing that I couldn't or shouldn't forgive her for. No matter what, I needed to make sure that she wasn't mad at me. I needed to make sure that I had her approval. This idea is what allowed me to keep loving her and not harbor ill feelings toward her. It's what made me want to keep trying.

When God revealed this to me, I started to see flashbacks of my childhood. I asked God how a mother-daughter relationship connected to the relationship between a man and a woman. How did it connect to friendships? *It's all about the cycle.* Well, I was given this analogy.:. Let's use a wash cycle for example. If you wash a load of white clothes and add a red item to the wash, you can end up with a load of pink clothes after the wash is over. Sometimes you put the white clothes in the cycle again, add more detergent and increase the bleach- all with the intention of ridding the clothes of the pink stain. When the clothes are out of the wash cycle, you notice that the stain is still there. Instead of throwing the clothes away, you decide to embellish your favorite piece and wear the others around the house or under other garments. Though you made adjustments, you never fixed the problem. The problem was either masked or hidden.

Well, the emotionally impactful experiences that I had in my childhood followed me to adulthood because they were never resolved. I carried them for years. I masked and embellished the hurt and void with smiles, laughs and vulnerability. I tried my best to move forward but when I tried, it didn't work. Just like with re-washing the clothes, there was still a stain. I made an association with acceptance that was based on a child's perception of love. These emotionally impactful experiences were with both friends and my mother. By no means am I saying that my mother never loved me. I know that she did. What I am saying is that I never learned how to accept rejection from those that I loved and move on, how to deal with and learn from hurt, or how to disassociate myself from those who did not appreciate me. I didn't talk to my mom much about the things that I was dealing with as an adolescent. The one time I tried talking to her about relationship issues as a young adult, her response left me feeling like I should have kept it to myself. So, instead of me learning how to cope with issues, I suppressed them and held on.

I felt like anyone who held a space in my heart (friend, family, significant other, etc.) deserved all of me no matter how they treated me. My ability to take and accept whatever they said or did was cultivated as a child. I applied the concept that regardless of how harsh what they did was, there was nothing that I couldn't or shouldn't forgive them for. Which still holds true. We must forgive! Not for others but for ourselves, our sanity and our salvation. The problem was that I considered those relationships and friendships to be on the same level as that of the relationship with my mother. Why? Because I was missing those teachings and experiences to help me make the connection and the separation. I didn't have many friends growing up, so I didn't have much practice in that area. I needed some things that only my mother could provide. There was a void. It wasn't until the revelation that I knew I was filling a void and placing people in a space that was never intended for them.

When I was in a relationship with Shawn, it was the first of its kind. It was my first introduction to love in a relationship with a man. The connection was like no other. I was vulnerable. I let him in. I felt accepted. I felt safe. I was happy. Even when I talked to him about things that I experienced with my friends and my mother, or when he heard it for himself, he calmed my spirit and I felt secure. (I felt these same emotions as a young child with my mother. The insecurity I felt in my relationship with mother didn't happen until I was a little older.) Like I said before, I know that she loved me. She nurtured me but as in any relationship, there were some gaps. Oddly, I subconsciously made a connection between the relationship with my mom and the one with Shawn. When my relationship with Shawn ended, the void was still there and it was filled with toxic relationships with other men, unwise business decisions and short-lived friendships. Until this revelation, I thought that the void I felt was solely because of Shawn's absence. But I was wrong. *It was all about the cycle!*

Another part of my revelation was that I was always drawn to people who had large families. In awe, I would sometimes watch them interact with each other. I wanted to be able to tell the Auntie and Uncle jokes. I wanted a close bond with my cousins. I wanted to be able to say that I would do anything for my family. But my family was broken. I wanted a family so badly that I stayed in an abusive marriage just so I wouldn't have a broken family. However, the family I created was broken the moment abuse began. For a while, I blamed Shawn for my poor choices in men. I was upset with how he left me, and I honestly felt like the reason why I "took wooden nickels" was because of my tainted first experience of love with him. I had to suck it up and own up to my own decisions. I can say that he did shape a part of my outlook on relationships, but the decisions that were made were ALL MINE.

I had to be comfortable with the fact that I failed. Though failure was never my intention, it was often a result and I had to own up to it. I had to embrace the fact that I said yes to every relationship that I was in. I chose to stay when all signs pointed to GET AWAY! I chose to commit to friendships that were obviously unhealthy. I stopped believing in myself. I stopped encouraging myself. I stopped taking care of myself. I allowed people to form a wedge between me and my children. I made poor financial decisions. I chose to involve myself with people that were not a part of my destiny. EVERYTHING led back to me.

When we begin to take ownership of our lives, we will often find out that the issue is us. Yes, experiences lead up to certain decisions. Yes, exposure contributes to personal pain and trauma. Yes, other people can do things and say things that damage us and pierce our hearts so deeply that occasionally, we unexpectedly feel the sting of the wound. However, and again, EVERYTHING leads back to the individual making the decisions- YOU, ME, US.

We must stop blaming others for our pain and suffering. The fact of the matter is that once the infliction is over, we have control of the next step, the next moment, the next move. We must decide that enough is enough. We must push ourselves to freedom in our minds and our souls. Remember, after the pain and suffering, the next step is on YOU.

I decided to stop the cycle that I was in. I decided to stop masking and embellishing my mess. I decided to start over. One thing that I have learned over time, is that there is a moment called the future and the present does not last long. I cannot relive or change the past, but I can put 100% of effort into my next moment. Yes, I was hurt by men. Yes, I had an imperfect relationship with my mother. Yes, I had a broken family. Yes, I had unhealthy friendships.

However, instead of dwelling on those "Yes" experiences and decisions, I chose to start declaring my "No's". I would say to myself: "No, I will not allow pain to overtake me. No, I will not allow negative thoughts to plague me. No, I will not blame myself for what others have done to me. No, I will not allow someone to use me. No, I will not allow the devil to make me think I failed at everything I have done. No, I will not live in the past". Why? Because the cycle must be broken, and it begins with me. I will embrace every "it" in my life with the selfish intent to be a better woman, wife, mother, entrepreneur, steward, and educator. Because I shifted my thoughts…because I made a decision…because I decided to forgive and love myself again…because I decided to no longer embellish and mask my "it's"…because I decided to talk to and trust God…

THE CYCLE HAS ENDED!

PART TWO:

THE

METHOD

THE EMBRACE METHOD

7 STEPS TO EMBRACING & RELEASING YOUR "IT"

As you have learned and as I have shared, throughout my life I struggled in the areas of friendship, love and relationship. But I also struggled with self-care. It started as a young girl wanting so badly to be "a part of" that I found myself accepting people and things that were unhealthy for me. All because I was harboring thoughts, emotions, and ideas that were fueled by failure and nurtured by despair; thus, resulting in me not always taking care-mental care, emotional care, sexual care, spiritual care-of myself as I became an adult.

When I came to the realization that there were areas in my life that I was afraid to embrace but needed to overcome, I was faced with having to make a decision. My decision could not be predicated upon someone else's timing, nor could it be contingent upon someone else's approval. It had to be based solely on a decision that I made, and I had to make it **ALONE**. I do not mean alone in the sense that God wasn't with me or on my side. I mean alone as in not leaning on another person's suggestion or advice. It was just me and God.

You see, I had a fear of loneliness. It was not to the extent that I hungered to seek friendships, relationships, companionships or professional advancements. But I struggled with letting go of what I chose to connect myself to because I had a fear of being disconnected. I feared the reality of no longer having what I had. For so long, I felt like I had a responsibility to remain loyal even when loyalty wasn't reciprocated. This concept led to the demise of my view of my worth.

While journeying through embracing the things that hindered me from loving myself, believing in myself or enjoying my life's triumphs, I found out that doing it alone was not only necessary in order to revive my view of my worth, it was also a vital part of my mental health.

God took me through a *7-step process of embracing* my issues which led to my deliverance. This process, (The Method I mentioned earlier), caused me to accept the fact that releasing those things that kept me from experiencing deliverance and freedom was my responsibility. I had to take the steps. I had to accept what was discovered. I had to make the needed adjustments so that ***I could remain free***.

I was freed from anxiety. I was freed from fear. I was freed from regret. I was freed from self-blame. I released it all and I let God lead.

In this part of the book, you must be ready and committed to release, to change and to forgive. Moving forward with *The Method* means there is no turning back! Relax, breathe and BE SET FREE!

This method worked for me when I needed/wanted to be delivered from things that hindered me. I think that it will work for you, and I hope that you will try it too. I call it the EMBRACE Method.

Evaluate
Make a decision
Believe you can
Release your "IT"
Activate your inner strength
Create a plan
Execute the plan

If you have made it to this page, it means that you have made a decision to RELEASE YOUR "IT's"! I commend you for taking the initiative to be released from the things that have hindered you from progressing in life. Get your pen and paper ready (or use the notes pages at the end of this book)! Embrace and enjoy the process. After all, YOU ARE WORTH IT!

STEP 1

EVALUATE

What is your "IT"? Your "IT" is anything that causes you to feel anxiety, anger, fear, depression, sadness, confusion or any emotion that negatively impacts your personal and spiritual growth.

In this step, you must ask yourself and answer some important questions. You will be creating an "IT" list.

<u>Action:</u> On a separate sheet of paper, answer the following:

> What is your "IT"? (This will be answered in the form of a list. Further instructions are below.)

> Why is it your "IT"?

> When did it become your "IT"?

> Where does your mind, spirit or heart travel to when you reflect on your "IT"?

Your "IT" list can be as short or as long as it needs to be. This is YOUR list. Take your time to be honest with yourself and think about what it is that has been holding you back. At this moment, I suggest that you also use this time to pray. Talk to God and ask Him to reveal to you the things that have been blocking you. Sometimes, we can only see what we allow ourselves to see but when the Holy Spirit reveals things to us, it is without bias or ill intent. It's as raw as it can get. Embrace the emotions that may come and release them to God. I promise you, He can handle it!

STEP 2

MAKE A DECISION

Brethren, I count not myself to have apprehended: but this
one thing I do, forgetting those things which are behind, and
reaching forth unto those things which are before.
Philippians 3:13 KJV

In this step, you must decide to put your "IT"
behind you. You must make a decision to be released
and move forward. If you fail to decide to release
yourself from your "IT", you will find yourself stuck in a
place of pain and discomfort. The hardest part of
getting over your "IT" is the starting point of getting
through your "IT". Decide to start TODAY.

Reflect on the answers from Step 1 and decide on
what you need to be released from. Are you deciding
to release yourself from the anxiety associated with
your "IT"? Are you deciding to be released from
bitterness or unforgiveness associated with your "IT"?
Really think about what has been weighing you down.
Do not be afraid of a long list. Do not feel discouraged
by how much you need to be released from. Whether
there are 2 things or 50 things on your list, the beauty
in this is the RELEASE! Keep the release as your
focus.

Action: On the same sheet of paper that you used
for Step 1, write down what you are deciding to
release yourself from.
Example: *Question from Step 1: What is your "IT"?*
Answer: My IT is my father.
Step 2: I need to be released from the hatred that I
have towards my father.

STEP 3

BELIEVE YOU CAN

I will praise thee; for I am fearfully and wonderfully made:
marvellous are thy works; and that my soul knoweth right well.
Psalm 139:14 KJV

When you believe, there is a sense of assurance that exists that is hard to diminish. Believe that you can move forward. Believe that you are worthy of having the best. Believe that you are fearfully and wonderfully made. Being fearfully and wonderfully made means that you were made in the image of God. He is perfect and He made no mistakes with you. You were made in the image of a God who is so wonderful and so amazing that one should be fearful of having just a thought that He erred in creating you. Why should one be fearful of that thought? Because God is so great and there is none greater than Him. We were created to please God and we should only fear to displease such an awesome God. He is so powerful and there is none more powerful than Him. Because of who He is, to question His greatness, His power or His perfection is simply the wrong choice to make.

I was at a point in my life when I did not believe that I could forgive Shawn for leaving me or my ex-husband for spitting in my face, embarrassing me in front of people, hitting me or even cheating on me. I did not believe that I could love or be loved again. I did not believe that I could be hired for a job that would pay me decent money. I did not believe that I could have a friend that I could trust. I did not believe that I could ever look in the mirror and like what I saw.

Once I took the step to be released from those things, thoughts, emotions and lies that the devil planted in my mind, I then made a conscious decision to believe that I could move forward and have what I desired and deserved. I had to cry my way through my thoughts and even yell at the devil when I began to think that I could not. Believing you can live a happy life after life makes it look like you can't, isn't easy. But I did it. Which means it is possible. If I did it, so can you! BELIEVE!

*This step is a very important step. If you don't believe that you can move forward and be released from your "IT", the rest of this method will be difficult. I am not solely talking about this very moment. I'm talking about in the midnight hour, days, weeks, even months down the line, when the devil tries to torment your mind and place fear and doubt in your spirit. The belief that you are declaring in this moment must be sustained in order for you to persevere in those moments.

Action: Right now, I want you to create a personal "I CAN" statement.

You can use the notes paper provided for you or something else of your choosing. Don't write this statement on any old piece of paper. Be intentional with what you choose to write it on. Why? Because what you are about to declare is special, powerful, meaningful and impactful and you deserve to look at this "I CAN" statement and be proud of what is says.

You will use this "I CAN" statement whenever that hour, day, week or month comes when the devil tries to cause you to believe that you can't move forward or that you have not been delivered.

This "I CAN" statement needs to include words and phrases that speak positivity and encouragement. Words and phrases like: wonderful, amazing, go-getter, survivor, never give up, God said so, and the devil is a liar, to name a few.

STEP 4

Release your "IT"

Be careful for nothing; but in every thing by prayer and supplication with thanksgiving let your requests be made known unto God. And the peace of God, which passeth all understanding, shall keep your hearts and minds through Christ Jesus.
Philippians 4:6-7 KJV

After you have evaluated your "IT", release everything connected to it. The things that hinder us become hindrances because of how we think. Yes, an outward experience may have created a moment that we need to embrace. But choose to think of it as such- a moment that needs to be embraced, not as a hindrance. When we shift our way of thinking, we also change our approach to our negative or impactful experiences. These events are only identified as a hindrance AFTER you have thought of it as one. Once you begin to think of things as a hindrance or a blockage, you begin to feel like you are defeated. Once it goes from your mind to your heart, you begin to walk in it. Today, you will become free in your mind, free in your heart and free to walk in your purpose. Go ahead. Release the pain, the anger, the anxiety, the fear or whatever your "IT" is. RELEASE IT. Allow the peace of God which passeth all understanding to keep you.

Do this release activity:

Items Needed: One black balloon, an index card

<u>Action 1</u>: Either order or go to the local party store and get a black balloon. Why black? Because black is typically worn at funerals. The archetypal meaning of black is death, sadness, doom and the like. For the most part, nothing about it is designed to be positive in nature (with the exception of black skin of course-wink).

<u>Action 2</u>: Get the balloon filled with helium.

<u>Action 3</u>: On an index card or a small piece of paper, write down EVERYTHING that you are releasing today (refer to the responses from Step 2). Be specific. Be detailed.

<u>Action 4</u>: After you are done, staple the index card/paper to the top of the balloon string.

<u>Action 5</u>: Go outside. (Going to the place where you experienced your "IT" is suggested but not required).

<u>Action 6</u>: In this step, you will be releasing the negative. This release is more like a ceremony. You are ridding yourself of what once hindered you. Your "IT's" funeral is today.

Right before you release your "IT" into the sky, declare the following:

I am no longer bound by (state everything that you listed).

On today (state the month, day and year), I release everything that has been weighing me down.

I release everything that has hindered me from progressing.

Lord, the battle in my mind, in my heart, belongs to you. This battle is not mine; it is Yours. Because I have given the battle to You, I am no longer bound by it. In fact, the battle is already won. I am on the side called victory.

I am not an advocate for defeat.

From this day forward, I move in purpose and NOT in fear!

Action 7: Release the balloon and watch it until you see it no more. (*This is a good time to Give God Glory for your release, to tell God "Thank You", or just soak it all in with peace at the forefront of your mind.*)

Action 8: Now say: **(Your name), you did it! You Embraced your "IT"!**

STEP 5

Activate Your Inner Strength

A merry heart doeth good like a medicine: but a broken spirit
drieth the bones.
Proverbs 17:22 KJV

At this step in the process, you just have to **DO**.

Action: Set a day aside where you take at least one hour for yourself.

It may have to be late at night or early in the morning. It would be best if you completed this step right after completing Step 4. Besides, you just accomplished a lot and you deserve this moment with yourself. However, if you cannot, don't stress. This is the perfect accountability opportunity. Make sure to set the time to complete Step 5 within THE NEXT 7 DAYS- no later. This is important. You must set the momentum. The time of day doesn't matter. All that matters is that you **DO**. You can choose what to do. You deserve this time for yourself. Treat yourself to whatever you need or want. When you feel better, you do better but when your spirit is broken and sad, it's difficult to do much of anything. So, relax, eat some chocolate, watch TV, pray, whatever suits your needs, **DO IT**.

This step is not a one-time thing. Make time for yourself regularly, preferably at least once a week. Sometimes this step can be uncomfortable, especially if you're not used to taking time out for yourself. It's ok. Trust me. You'll get used to it. In the meantime, if the idea of frequency is a concern, or this step is a little overwhelming, start with taking time out once a month and work your way to once a week until you find the frequency that works for you.

Make sure that you reverence God during this personal time. Though this time is "for you", it is about Him, too. If you are reading this book, God has given you the time. You have to choose to make it your personal time with just you and God. This time is needed to activate your inner strength and in order for you to activate your inner strength, you need to tap into Him. He IS your inner strength. While relaxing and taking time out to "reset", allow Him in. Talk to Him, pray to Him. It is in Him that your strength lies but it is up to you to keep it activated. You accomplish this through the intimate time that you spend with Him. This step is a gentle reminder of your worth. Don't replace prayer time with this time. They are completely different.

Here's what I mean: During prayer time, you are directly focused on interaction or conversation with God. It is a time to ask God for clarity, help, or even intercession. Prayer time is also a time when you can worship God. The focus during prayer time, unlike the time that this step is referring to, requires you to be completely selfless. Your focus is not solely on you. Your request can be about you (your need for peace, forgiveness or clarity), but your primary focus is to reach Him.

KEEP YOUR INNER STRENGTH ACTIVATED BY REGULARLY TAKING TIME OUT FOR YOURSELF AND REVERENCING GOD IN THE PROCESS.

TAKE CARE OF YOURSELF.

YOU DESERVE IT AND YOU'VE EARNED IT.

MOVE ON TO STEP 6 <u>ONLY</u> AFTER COMPLETING STEP 5

STEP 6
CREATE A PLAN

Ye are of God, little children, and have overcome them:
because greater is he that is in you, than he that is in the world.
1John 4:4 KJV

What will you do to ensure that you do not revert to your old way of thinking and feeling? Do you state daily affirmations? Do you clear your "closet" (the hidden things)? Do you disconnect from people and things that are still connected to or reminders of your "IT"?

How will you remain focused on your new venture? Do you walk with confidence? Do you keep your head up?

Well, you will do whatever it takes. There may be multiple things that you need to do.

<u>Action:</u> Whatever your "IT" was, create a plan that contradicts everything about "IT" and write it down.

If it was fear, declare peace and create a plan to maintain peace. If there was doubt, speak assurance and create a plan to maintain that assurance. Because you have vowed to keep your inner strength activated and told God that you released your "IT" to Him, you are no longer bound by the emotion connected to it. The God that resides in you is greater than anything or anyone in this world that has hindered you. For these reasons, you are free to think clearly about your plan.

There is no specific special plan. The great thing about this step is that the plan you create is tailored to your needs. It is created just for you. I had to create multiple plans. All the "IT's" in my life did not require the same course of action. When I had to embrace and release the fact that I had issues with disconnecting from people, I had to create a plan that included an affirmation that I memorized. I spoke that affirmation at the very moment I began to feel like I had to accept how a person negatively treated me or prove to them that I was loyal when it was clear that I needed to disconnect myself from them. When I had to embrace doubt and fear of my worth, I created a plan that required me to keep a running record of my successes, be it big or small, and reward myself for my accomplishments. The reward would be a nice lunch, a luxury pedicure, lengthy nap or whatever I wanted at the moment.

Write the vision and make it plain! Keep the plan posted where you can see it daily. Sometimes we just need a reminder that we made a commitment and have a plan that will work.

STEP 7
Execute the Plan

For God hath not given us the spirit of fear; but of power,
and of love, and of a sound mind.
2Timothy 1:7 KJV

MOVE FORWARD!

DON'T STOP!

KEEP PUSHING!

KEEP BELIEVING!

DON'T BE AFRAID!

GOD GAVE YOU POWER! KEEP DECLARING!

FOLLOW THE PLAN!

<u>Action:</u> Recite the following affirmation:

**I woke up today not to complain, but to be the
change that I want to see.**

**I look at myself and see positive change in
me.**

I will embrace every moment as an opportunity to complete my assignment and strengthen my role in this world.

I have the power to influence.

Difficult times come, but they also go.

Mistakes happen, but I possess the ability to correct those mistakes.

I am (state your name) and I have embraced and conquered my "IT".

Because I dared to try, opened my heart, let God lead and created a plan, I can go out into the world and EMBRACE IT.

NOTES

NOTES

Girrrrrl, You Embraced IT!

I pray that you realize the magnitude of what you just did! Just in case you don't, let me tell you. You just used the power that God gave you! God gave you power over the enemy. He gave you access to Him through prayer and that same prayer is a weapon against the schemes, attacks and tricks of the enemy (the devil). You just opened up space in your heart so God can do what He does- fill you up with more of Him. You just made yourself available to receive the things that God has stored up for you. What are those things? They are everything you need and the things that are in the will of God that you desire.

Girl, YOU JUST DID SOMETHING HUGE!

Things to remember as you continue this journey:

- ✓ *Remember your "I CAN" statement. Remember to state your affirmations. Remember to keep these posted where you can see them.*

- ✓ *Remember to also keep your plan posted up.*

- ✓ *Remember to revisit Step 5 every week.*

- ✓ *Remember that you may have to follow these 7 steps multiple times, depending on where life takes you- and that's okay.*

- ✓ *But most importantly, remember that God made no mistakes with you. You are fearfully and wonderfully made and because you dared to try, opened your heart, let God lead you and created a plan, now you can go out into the world and EMBRACE IT!*

About The Author

Shalimar Johnson comes to you from the State of Georgia by way of Miami, Florida. She is a daughter, sister, mother and wife. She enjoys shopping, event planning and going to the theatre. She loves God and His people and has set out to make sure that she impacts the lives that God has assigned to her to the best of her ability.

She is also a scholar who has earned a Film & T.V. Conservatory certification, Associates in Medical Assistant, Bachelor's in Social Science w/ an Education Concentration, Master's in Education and a Master's in Psychology. After high school, Shalimar attended The School for Film & Television Conservatory College in NYC. After graduating, at 20 years old, Shalimar moved to California to pursue an acting career. While booking acting jobs, she also attended college to earn a degree in education. She had little money and a lot of adult responsibilities (bills, food, shelter, car, etc.) but she did not give up. She was constantly booking jobs, meeting influential people in the industry, attending industry parties and rapidly progressing in her craft. However, she wasn't able to keep up financially and ended up homeless and living out of her car.

Shalimar decided to try and start over again, so she drove all the way from California to Florida with a goal to return to California but, Shalimar was faced with another challenge. One evening while driving from a friend's house, she was in a bad car accident and life as she knew it halted. She finally made it out of the spinal recovery rehabilitation center from a spinal cord injury that had her temporarily paralyzed and left there with a greater level of determination to win in life.

During her time in the hospital, she began to grow closer to God. Her desire for her life started to become more Christ-centered. She loved acting but started to feel like maybe God allowed the accident because she was moving too fast in the acting industry. She began to feel like God blocked something that would have been detrimental to her life. She wanted to fulfill God's purpose for her life- whatever that was.

As time progressed, she became a single mother raising a son. She decided to go back to school and juggle bills, motherhood and life. During this time, due to her high level of determination, she started an organization called "Find Your Purpose, Embrace Your Destiny" where people ages 12 and up, who were seeking God, could connect with like-minded people and receive support and insight while on their journey.

Several years later, she got married to a man that she thought would be the perfect husband and father. He was a preacher (later became a Pastor during their marriage), he seemed to love God, her and her son. During this marriage, Shalimar had her second child. That marriage was rough because of the constant physical and verbal abuse (this story is the focus of one of her next books).

Aside from all of those experiences and struggles, Shalimar still leaned on God and in 2010, she was ordained as a minister. The marriage to the Pastor ended but Shalimar kept pressing on. Now a divorced single mother of two children from two different men, Shalimar really wanted to prove to herself and other women that life didn't end because life did what life does. She started "My Scars Are Beautiful", an organization designed to encourage, empower and pray for women and children who are survivors of domestic violence. She held annual empowerment events with this goal in mind.

She took a chance on love and got married again. During this marriage she had her third child, became an entrepreneur and owns *Faces of Expression*- a summer camp, started the Girl, Embrace IT! Movement and created the SatHERday's w/ Shalimar J Talk Show which airs on Network TV. She is dedicated to empowering women across the globe to trust God, embrace the moments that life brings, release all hindrances and FORGIVE.

You can follow or reach Shalimar at:

 INSTAGRAM:

@GIRLEMBRACEIT

 FACEBOOK:

SHALIMAR JOHNSON

GIRL EMBRACE IT TV

CHRISTIAN WOMEN NETWORK

WEBSITE: WWW.GIRLEMBRACEIT.COM